PLAIN AND SIMPLE WISDOM

april
1995

To Jo
With Love
& Friendship

Beverly

PLAIN

and

SIMPLE

WISDOM

SUE BENDER

Illustrations by
Sue and Richard Bender

HarperSanFrancisco
A Division of HarperCollins*Publishers*

First Edition

Library of Congress Cataloging-in-Publication Data

Bender, Sue
    Plain and Simple Wisdom / Sue Bender.—1st ed.
        p. cm.
    ISBN 0-06-251174-2 (pbk : alk. paper)
    1. Conduct of life—Quotations, maxims, etc. 2. Simplicity—Quotations, maxins, etc. 3. Aphorisms and apothegms. 4. Amish—Miscellanea I.Title.
BJ1581.2.B4384 1995
170'.44—dc20   94-38418
                                                               CIP

95 96 97 98 99 ❖ HAD 10 9 8 7 6 5 4 3 2 1

This edition is printed on acid-free paper that meets the American National Standards Institute Z39.48 Standard.

Book design by Gordon Chun Design

Perhaps each of us has a starved place, and each of us knows deep down what we need to fill that place. To find the courage to trust and to honor to search, to follow the voice that tells us what we need to do, even when it doesn't seem to make sense, is a worthy pursuit.

To follow "a path that has a heart"—

to take it wherever it leads.

I set out on an unfamiliar path toward an unknown conclusion. I was hoping for answers, but I kept finding my way back to the question (the eternal question): "What really matters?"

We don't need reasons for doing what we do.

Learning to follow your heart is reason enough.

Those first old quilts I saw—proscribed, ordered, and intense—told me something about the women who made them and their view of the world.

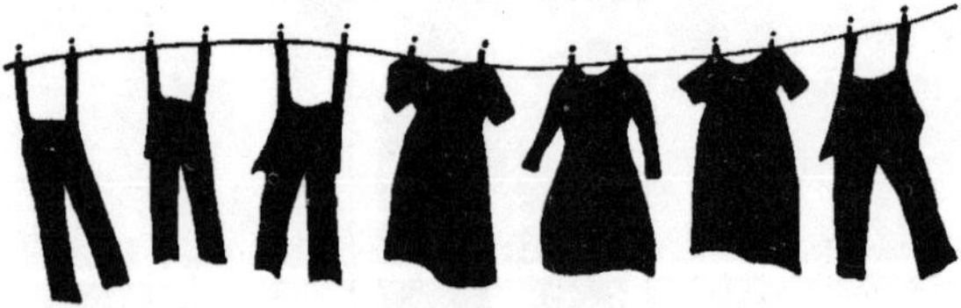

For the Amish, everything is a ritual.
Doing the dishes, mowing the lawn, baking bread,
quilting, canning, hanging out the laundry,
picking fresh produce, weeding—no distinction is
made between the sacred and the everyday.

Listening to your heart,

finding out who you are, is not simple.

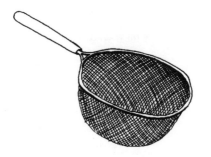

For the Amish, time is full and generous. The women move through the day unhurried. There is no rushing to finish, to get on to the important things. All work is important.

It takes a lot of courage to know who you are
and what you want.

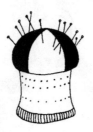

In the silence of "not doing" we begin

to know what we feel.

Sometimes we confuse what we do with

what we are.

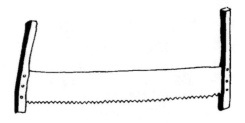

Any type of work can be meaningful.
It's the spirit in which you do it that
makes the difference.

An Amish woman told me,

"Making a batch of vegetable soup,

it's not right for the carrot to say

I taste better than the peas, or the pea to say

I taste better than the cabbage.

It takes all the vegetables to make a good soup!"

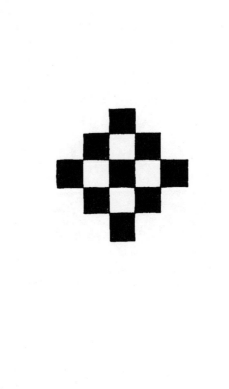

To simplify we have to say no.

The ordinary can be extraordinary.

For the Amish, making a doll or a quilt is no more special than canning green beans or making a cake.

Am I a successful human being, not only a success?

The Amish live what they believe.

Their life is their art.

Five minutes in the early morning and five minutes
in the evening were devoted to prayer.
The rest of the day was spent living their beliefs.
Their life was all of one piece. It was all sacred—
and all ordinary.

Our homes reflect who we are and what we value.

It's not rushing through tasks to achieve a series of goals that is satisfying, it's experiencing each moment along the way.

Order calms.

Accumulating choices is a way of not having to make a choice.

Lists engulf us—creating the illusion

that our lives are full.

Simplify and then go deeper,

making a commitment to what remains.

Satisfaction comes from giving up wishing we were doing something else—or being somewhere else.

When you seek to be special,

only a few things in life will measure up.

Nothing you are doing is wasted time.

There is a big difference between having many choices and making a choice.

Satisfaction comes from doing the work over and over—beginning to value a high standard.

When we are frantic and feel particularly rushed,

we can stop and ask, "Rushing for what?"

When the house is a mess, when there isn't a single

moment of calm, or the time to wash even one dish,

we can think of the tranquility of the Amish,

and realize we too have made a choice.

The need to be special and stand out,
the need for communality, to be part of the whole,
the hunger to belong, to be one among the many—
these equally competing, conflicting values are
part of each of us.

Piecing together our paradox—making peace with the paradox, finding a balance in some larger sense, so that life can feel whole.

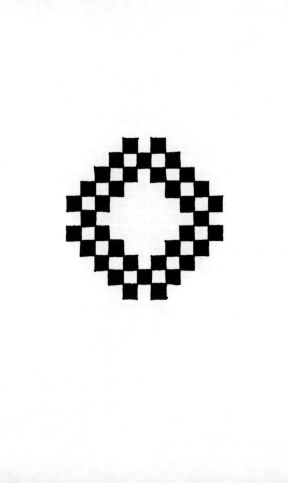

To reconcile our seeming opposites,
to see them as both, not one or the other,
is our constant challenge.

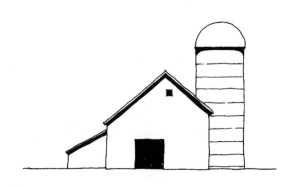

It's time to celebrate the lives we have.

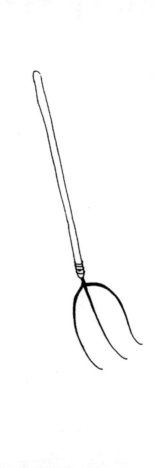

And we have another choice—

to accept what we didn't get to choose.

What's important is doing the best we can,

not being the best.

There is an old me, a new me, an imperfect me, and

the beginning of a new acceptance of all the me's.

Continue working on your "quilt."
It will tell you something about the life you've lived
and the things you've come to value.

Live what you believe—

make your whole life your art.

I had been looking for certainty,

and was finding comfort in uncertainty.

Leave room for the unexpected.

Learning to trust,

no matter what life turns out to be,

is a great discovery.

If we listen and hear what is being offered—

anything in life can be a guide.

There is a spirit guiding us, in ways we often don't
understand and don't need to understand.

What we are learning is often not what we expected.

What we are learning doesn't stay with us

all the time—we have glimpses, then it slips away.

Not knowing, and learning to be comfortable with not knowing, is a great discovery.

Miracles come after a lot of hard work.